Teach, Flourish, Thrive

Break Free From Burnout:
Seven Keys to Reignite Your
Passion for Teaching

Rowena Hicks

Book Cover and Illustrations by Olly Spring

Second edition 2024

P.S. Rowena Hicks loves to hear from fans! Reach out to her at authorrowenahicks@gmail.com

Acknowledgements

My 4 kids – Jamie, Jack, Olly and Abs, who have always been my inspiration and encouragement to believe in myself.

Sophie- chief editor and encourager- you gave me the courage for the first YouTube video and look what came next! Thank you!

Olly – artist extraordinaire! So much talent, you are my creative genius!

Emma, Karen and John SS- those who dealt with my terrible grammar! You are amazing.

Mum and dad – Thanks for all your faith in me!

My siblings – Emma, Paul and Amy, I love you guys.

Wings- you know who you are. Without you this would never have happened!

So many friends and colleagues who have been part of this journey. Thank you!

Punchy book accountability partners- Joan and Paul – our weekly meetings have been a lifeline, thank you so much!

My Hillsong community – who rescued me, I love doing life with you all.

My amazing niece Jess, who helped me out and was so determined to be on this list!

Contents

Introduction

Why you should read this book and why you can't afford not to!

Jim Rohn said: "Either you run the day or the day runs you"

Over the years, I've always told colleagues "You need to look after yourself as no one else is going to do it for you!" This is a truth I stand by- the problem was that I didn't apply it to myself!

Do you work in a school? Wonder if you will get through today? You rush, juggle, plan, prepare, scoop up whoever needs it, go over and above to do whatever is required…..need I go on? Whatever your role, many school staff are overwhelmed and heading for burnout. This is NOT OK!

I wrote this book after an episode of burnout. I loved my job but worked too hard, trying to help everyone while not looking after myself, or not even stopping to consider this might be needed!
I have worked in schools for over 30 years. I've been a teacher, specialist teacher, senco, tutor for the national award, and ended up a deputy head. I loved all my roles. I've worked mainly in

primary but also in two all through schools and an orphanage. I have a masters in inclusive education and have worked with some truly inspirational colleagues, but none of these protected me from myself!

This book is a simple, step by step guide towards understanding yourself and your colleagues better and finding ways to overcome the barriers that staff face every day. There are practical strategies to try, alongside mindset shifts and I hope to challenge your assumptions, habits and routines.

You will consider WHY you do this job, the impact you have and how to find ways to flourish amidst the busyness. You will discover your values and your strengths and how these combine to enable you to thrive. You will look at the relationships you have, what you contribute and what others offer- how to improve these team dynamics. You will also look at how to prioritise, adjust habits and mindsets to find better ways to be productive.

Overall, you know that unless you are happy, you are not as creative. If you are exhausted, you can't give out as you are empty. If you don't feel "seen" you lose motivation. We look at ways to readdress the balance.

If you want to start to understand how you can take back even a small amount of control in your day, this is a book for you. It's about learning to thrive instead of simply survive- to reignite your passion for teaching. Remember when you started in school? Enthusiastic, energetic, creative and fulfilled? Together we can re-capture that!

Download FREE Resources

Throughout this book, we will mention different resources. You can use the website and QR code below to access them.

subscribepage.io/dcmU0z

Chapter 1

The reality and the challenge. Discover the impact of investing in yourself.

I thought I was having a heart attack! I had walked downstairs on Sunday morning and suddenly had to call to my child to help me out. I was dizzy with chest pain and other pains shooting round my body. Next thing I knew there were a couple of paramedics in the house, checking me out and I was telling them I was so sorry to be making such a fuss, that I was fine; but they insisted I go in the ambulance to hospital. It turned out not to be a heart attack: it was stress, exhaustion and a warning of possible burn out that I didn't heed. After a few days off, I went back to working long hours, trying to find my worth in working harder, achieving more, making a difference, driving myself further...

That was me two years ago. Two years later and I have had to resign as the symptoms came back, stronger this time and more consistent. I LOVED my job. I loved the children, the staff, working with the families. I'd been a special needs coordinator (SENco), then climbed to deputy Head where I believed I could support staff more and make a greater impact. Looking back, I worked so hard, and thought about work when I wasn't there. I think it became so much a matter of WHO I was, not just what I did. Perhaps this is because I see working in school as a vocation, not just a job. You?

That was why I ended up shaving a bald patch in my child's hair! More of that in Chapter 6!

This is the situation for so many staff in so many schools both from my experience, and from what I have read. Do any of these issues resonate with you?

- Too much to do and overloaded
- Not enough time
- Lacking confidence for the range and scale of tasks required
- Being observed/judged/graded... (depending on your school approach)
- Juggling priorities
- Never finishing a task properly
- Feeling like a fraud - will you be found out?
- Not sure what you are doing from moment to moment
- Lacking energy

Now add your own:

-
-
-
-

From day to day, amongst the busyness, I would oscillate between any of the above! Perhaps we all do?

I LOVE working in schools. It is my passion and my joy. I assume you do too, but like me, you are exhausted and hoping to find some tools to add to your armoury to give you strength for the term ahead. I've been searching for years for ways to approach my job better and to help others around me to do the same.

Through the book you will look at

- The positive impact you have on the children - potential for feedback - watch for it!
- The impact of investing in yourself, discovering your strengths, becoming a better version of yourself
- Responding to challenge & having the courage to be imperfect
- Self-awareness - do you actually have it? What is it really? Does it matter?
- Workload and using time wisely - there are even solutions here!
- Your team, relationships, feedback you receive and give, being "seen"
- Finding your value from another place - within

This book is for the brave, determined and courageous person who is prepared to accept that there may be adjustments to how they see life, do life, want life and think about life. Then to take the steps to try something new or even make some small adjustments.

My goal for you

Brene Brown says that vulnerability is our most accurate measurement of courage. Writing this book is, for me, laying bare my weakness, my mistakes, my joys, in the hope it helps someone become a better, more empowered version of themselves. That is my goal - for you to see your value, and in understanding this, to become inwardly strong, resilient, confident, fulfilled, energetic, even happy! I'd be content with one or two of these things!

To take this journey with me, you will need to be vulnerable with yourself, stay teachable (we are all always learning, right?) and take the wins. There may be some things that don't resonate with you, or you try and they don't work - that's fine! Turn the page to the next idea!

Do you feel stuck? Powerless? Exhausted? Empty? Excited? Driven? Optimistic?... this book is for you!

Getting the most from this book

This book is for you if you want to find the best version of yourself and walk into what this means. It is a book of action steps, trial and error and of sharing your mistakes and victories! That's how we learn best. But first you have to try! I've been to so much training which is brilliant and I forgot most of it when I left the room. I'm hoping that if you apply some of the activities, they will embed and make more of a difference. Dr Chapman in his book *The 5 Love Languages* points out that written words have the benefit of being read over and over again. As you write down where you are at, try out strategies, see your development, note it down, that in itself is so encouraging, even empowering. It might feel a bit unnecessary, but try it, you may be surprised.

This is an interactive book with questions asked and tables to complete. If you have an e-reader rather than a physical book you may want to go through with a note book, ensuring that you write notes to make it clear to yourself to go back through later. Of course, you may be one of those people who skim through, looking for what resonates with you. No problem. My hope is that each person who reads this book will find nuggets to encourage, empower, energise and give you hope.

Each section will give you some background, something to ponder and then action steps. I'm a great believer in watching for impact and positives from each attempt! Remember we don't necessarily learn in a linear, ordered fashion. We try different approaches and see what works for each one of us!

We will look at why it matters that you understand your value, from personal experience and from research. Then consider the impact of understanding this and what we can do about it, together!

Do any of these scenarios resonate with you? Tick any boxes...

1. I started in a school where the teaching assistants lined up outside my office to explain individually how desperate they were. They felt no one listened to them, they'd had so little training, no support, few resources and yet pressure to demonstrate impact.

2. I was teaching a Maths lesson to a class of eight boys in an alternative provision. It was very practical and quite noisy. I was so engrossed in the lesson that I didn't see the head of the Academy come in the back behind me and observe for a few minutes. I was told by the children after he left. My stomach lurched as if I was on a roller coaster - utter sense of being out of control / maybe some fear / what had he seen?

3. A special needs coordinator (SENco) in tears, explaining that they had spent three evenings at home writing a document to be told it wasn't good enough.

4. Seeing a parent so desperate and quite angry, appealing to me to help their child more, and feeling powerless to help.

5. I arrived in my class for the day as a supply teacher. Discovering a child was missing, the class gleefully informed me the child was up a tree nearby. What do you do when you have twenty nine eight year olds in a class, with the thirtieth up a tree?

What's the reality?

The reality in school is that you can never quite do enough, be enough and it's exhausting! There are so many demands and that is what makes it such a fun, dynamic and exciting place to work. Children and adults are different each day - what will today bring? We do what we do because we love children. We want what is best for them, and for them to be and achieve their full potential. Can we take that as a given? We spend hours discussing and working on helping the children, so now let's turn our eyes to ourselves. I challenge you to invest this little bit of time and see what changes you see.

Let's stop for a moment to think about **why you do this job?**

Can you list your own top 3 reasons? Your answers may be as simple as: Need an income, a job that fits with children, feel you have something to offer to children, love being with children...

1
2
3

When do you feel good at work?

So, if you now have your main reasons for doing this job, can you start to consider when during your day you feel at your best? Is this at the same time each day? Why? Same activity? Maybe it is certain reactions from children or adults (it could be role-dependent or task-dependent)? Other?

Fill out this grid, give it enough time. You may want to watch for the next few days, take notice, and complete it over the week... I'll tell you why this matters after you've had a go at completing the grid!

Day / Time	When I feel good:	Why do I think this is?
Eg 10.15am daily	Eg playtime	Eg I watch children happily playing and can help those who are isolated to be included

Why does this matter? There are so many reasons this is a good place to start when looking to find your best version of yourself. Firstly, if we start with the positives, you will start to notice more of them, and this is a simple win!

> **Top Tip** - Focus on and remember the positives!

It also matters because you are going to analyse your strengths as we go forward. You can match your strengths to the things that you love, in order to find how, where and when you might flourish (more on this later). If I tell you that when you feel drained, empty and exhausted, your brain takes you to negative places, does that resonate? However, if you feel exhausted and remember the wins in your day, where you have made a difference, this in itself is energising - try it out! Try it with one simple thing you have written above, focus on it tomorrow and see if it helps.

OK, so be brave! Let's start before we get going! Can you write where you currently think you get your value from? What helps you to believe in yourself?

Fill in the grid on the following page. **Remember, where you get your value from may not be the same as your strengths!**

Be as specific as you can: this is only for you!

What can you think of in your day that gives you a sense of worth, makes you buzz, feel good about yourself, feeling valued, that you have made a difference in some way?

For you this may be success, completing a task, words of affirmation, a child's hug, financial reward, feeling understood, being listened to, words of thanks, or something completely different.

Where do you THINK you get your **value** (sense of self-worth) from? Can you think of 6?

1	2	3
4	5	6

What does it mean to know your value?

The Cambridge Dictionary gives this as one of the definitions of VALUE: "The importance or worth of something or someone." Collins states, "The value of something such as a quality, attitude, or method is **its importance or usefulness**. If you place a particular value on something, that is the importance or usefulness you think it has."

Dr Chapman in his book on the 5 Love Languages suggests that many of us have received mixed messages about our worth. He suggests we all have a need for significance, we want our lives to count for something.

I suggest you have such extreme value, that the quest to discover your significance is well worth the curiosity, the energy, exploring what it means for you! What is your attitude to yourself? I wonder how you treat yourself? **Do you know your importance?**

Why me? I'm writing this book because I feel so strongly that you start to understand your self-worth. Once you do, you will become a better version of yourself. I found out about this firsthand, the hard way! In the past I never stopped to think about myself - how I needed to invest in myself to be able to be the best version of me. My journey has been a slow and messy climb through the ranks up to deputy headteacher, via a number of jobs in various schools, mainly within special needs. You will see through the book, as you get to know my story, that I rushed through life, not stopping to devote time to myself, invest in myself, with consequences.

I once watched as a teaching assistant (TA) was teaching a non-verbal child to communicate with cards and pictures. The TA looked so anxiously towards me, as if asking if she was doing the right thing. All I could see was a child so delighted to be learning to communicate how she felt, excitement on her face and wanting to have another go. Why don't we believe in ourselves and think we might be getting things right rather than wrong?

What is it about working in schools in the current climate that has resulted in so many lacking confidence in themselves and their skills, exhausted and feeling unseen?

Schools require standards, performance targets and consistency - all at a fast pace, ever changing, usually without sufficient resources. This results in pressure, juggling, rushing, and that's without considering anything that is going on at home for us all!

Over recent years, I've tried various strategies to help myself and those I have worked with to make small, but nevertheless important changes to their approach, attitude and actions so they have a better outcome to their day.

Top Tip - Start with small, achievable and measurable steps!

Why you need to read this book

It is a collection of strategies for busy and tired school staff to adopt in order to understand their value and hence improve their enjoyment, energy and productivity at work. Learning to be the best version of themselves.

Simply put: you are worth it! Take some time for you and watch what happens! Let's start with getting a bit uncomfortable and questioning ourselves. Denis D. Haack refers to the fact that "the most significant learning often involved or triggered discomfort as part of the process of growth." Are you prepared to come on this journey to look for strategies to find the best version of yourself? There may well be moments of discomfort - there certainly have been for me!

Chapter 2

Can you remember why you do the job? Don't underestimate your value.

Many years ago I was volunteering in a missionary school in East Africa. They had an eleven-year-old girl who was about to be excluded because she was so disruptive and defiant. She was refusing to engage with anything. I went to spend some time with her and learnt that she was pretty mad with everything in life. It didn't take long for me to discover that this was her sixth school as her parents moved round the world. As a result, she perceived herself to have failed everywhere and had no concept of how to make, or keep friends etc. We set up a simple programme of support, a buddy system, got her parents involved, all the things that seem obvious to you and me these days. Before long she was thriving. WHY? She felt seen and heard!

We all need a voice, children, adults, even school staff! Teaching assistants (TAs) tell me this really matters to them, and I'm sure it does to every member of the school community. I once asked a TA what helped her most during her week. She immediately responded that it was when I went and asked her how SHE was, not how her job was going, but a personal moment of recognition, checking up on how she really was. I would argue we all need this. To say how we are and how things are going. This builds relationship, reduces stress and you will work more effectively through your day.

Plenty of research shows that if we feel SEEN we are likely to be more productive. How can we make this happen more for ourselves and those we work with, whatever our roles?

<u>It is worth it!</u>

Earlier you considered why you do this job. You want to improve the lives of children, bring the best out in them, support them and their families. Or is it? Did you slip into it, or always wanted to do it?

Can you think back to an example of a time when you can remember thinking it was worth the effort, you saw the "win", remembered why you started out in this field?

My example is from when I led a six week parent/child club. The parents came into school and met with their child, so I could show them how we teach phonics and Maths skills to their children. The idea was that they could then better support their child at home. We had lots of fun with games. Then one session, two children were trying to work out a Maths problem and they suddenly GOT IT. It was a moment of realisation that they could achieve something, as if they could now conquer the world. I will not forget the look of delight on both those children's faces, nor the look on the faces of their parents. That is why I do the job!

> What's your example? A time you remembered why you do this job? What happened? Take your time to reflect on this, it's important!

You have a profound effect on the lives of the children you support (and the adults around you! More on that later!). It is rare, in my experience, to get much feedback from other adults in school, when we are all chasing our tail. Lovely when we do, of course, but perhaps our easiest win is to notice better where we make an impact on those around us ourselves.

Can I ask you who notices what you do? Do you feel SEEN? We get on with our jobs, work hard, do our best, does anyone recognise what you do?

1 win a day

Sometimes I think we go through the school day/week/term at such a fast pace that we don't stop to consider the impact we have. Are you aware of what you bring to your role? The wins, the joys, the difference you make?

Can you start a daily log of one win each day to remind yourself that you are having an impact? Try it for a week and see if this helps your sense of validation. This could come from anywhere during your day. This starts to remind you of your value and is very affirming. Simple yet effective!

For example, I told a parent that their child had been really kind in the playground that day, helping another child who had hurt himself. She was so pleased and told me that she had worried he didn't understand empathy and wasn't a kind child. She went away smiling. A one minute chat - huge impact! How did I feel? Satisfied: I'd achieved something that made a difference. Even a little good about myself! Interestingly, I have really struggled to identify in myself what the feelings were. Perhaps I can say it gave me a bit of a "buzz", or perhaps a chink of that sense of what it means to "flourish"? Can you identify with that at all?

Your example could be as simple as a teacher saying thanks to you for making up a task board that worked!

Day	What was the win?	How did you feel at that moment?
Monday		
Tuesday		
Wednesday		
Thursday		
Friday		

Of course, this can work both ways. Try looking for the value in others, in what they do and say. What is the impact on you and them?

I believe, from watching staff in school over the years, that we all bring so much more to the role than we know or realise. Can I take a moment to point out that during each day, you will have times when things do NOT work! That's OK too: it makes you and me human! Brene Brown says we need to have the courage to be imperfect. So let's accept now that this is our reality, and try not to focus on what went wrong but what worked! That way, we start to allow ourselves to thrive.

Top Tip- Focus on what worked!

Why does self-awareness matter so much?

How much do you know about self-awareness? I'm not just talking about introspection or self-analysis, but we need to become more aware that when we are not regulated, the children will pick this up and it is much harder to support them. Better self-awareness also tends to result in better wellbeing, being more fulfilled, more creative and more confident. I'll take that, please!

FACT CHECK - what percentage of people do you think are self-aware? Be honest and don't peep forward!

Your guess:

___%

FACT CHECK - 95 % of people think they are self-aware and the actual proportion of adults who are self-aware (according to research produced by Patricia Eulrich) is 10-15%!

Surprised? I was. I had thought I was quite self-aware, and the reality is that I'm probably NOT!

What can we do about it? Ask colleagues, see if they know the percentages. Are they self-aware, do you think? Talk about it as a team, raise it as a discussion as we want all of us to have the benefits of raised self-awareness mentioned above, don't we? But what even is self-awareness? The Oxford Learner's dictionary suggests that self-awareness is "conscious knowledge of one's own character and feelings."

In Patricia Eulrich's findings, the key ingredient that led some to having greater self-awareness was that they asked WHAT? instead of WHY?

This means that if you have a tricky meeting/chat/situation, ask yourself, '*What could I have done better?*' rather than, '*Why did that go wrong?*' This is a solution focused approach, which means you are looking to build rapid, desired change. I certainly want to become more self-aware if the advantages are greater wellbeing, confidence, creativity and fulfilment. I'm assuming if you have read this far that you want this too.

Let me tell you about a hospital visit with one of my own children. My son was about twelve and he was in a lot of pain. He has a bone condition that is very rare and the doctors at this hospital didn't yet know what it was. We were in the very lengthy process of finding a reason, a diagnosis. After a long wait with a very frustrated, angry pre-teen, we went in to see the specialist. Here was my son in the wheelchair and the doctor immediately told him for starters to get out of the wheelchair and stop making such a fuss. I was so angry I couldn't speak. I was shocked and horrified that a doctor would speak to a hurting child like this. I possibly didn't react very well at this point, reacting in anger and disbelief, muddling my words, spluttering I expect, and my son was the calmer version.

In retrospect, asking "What could I have done better to maintain a relationship and seek help from this hospital further?" would have had a better outcome than "Why did that go so wrong? Why didn't I react better? Why was he so apparently unhelpful?"

My son doesn't remember this incident over ten years ago, but I remember every moment clearly. I can now see that as I walked into that office I was already anxious so regulation went out the window at the lack of empathy and support. Improved self-awareness might have clocked my mood and then perhaps I could have more calmly discussed alternative avenues with him, rather than having to approach a different hospital.

The situation - where you used WHY?	Re-write it with your WHAT option

Life at home and school will bring situations where we have to react and we may not always get our reactions right in order to deliver the best outcome. We need to be realistic and honest with ourselves about this. However, if we can start analysing outcomes, it changes our thinking over time so we then manage situations better.

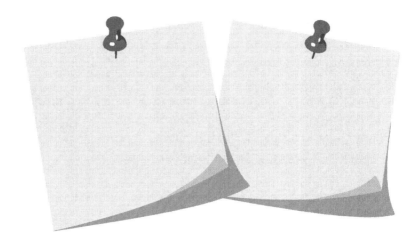

May I suggest (as a visual learner myself), that you get a post-it note, and write WHAT and WHY on it, then cross out the WHY as a reminder. See if you can apply this during the coming week - what is the result? Remember, this is about YOU finding strategies to empower YOU. Remember, research showed that those with better self-awareness had better wellbeing, were more fulfilled, could be more creative and even more confident. You want all of these, right?

Courage and imperfection

Let's think for a minute about home and school. The links are clear, i.e. if we have "stuff" going on at home, we have reduced capacity at work.

Brene Brown states that "if we are brave enough often enough, we will fall. These are the physics of vulnerability." Do we dare show a bit of vulnerability?

This is the same for children and adults. It comes back to being SEEN but also, as with children, do they/we dare (or have the opportunity) to share what is going on, to consider that they/we might need some support, time or resources just now?

I asked a teaching assistant one Monday how her packing had gone for her move that weekend, and her body language changed from hunched and exhausted, to smiling, more energetic/SEEN/valued/ thought of... get the point?

> **Top Tip** - Ask a colleague how they are, not about their work

I am NOT encouraging us all to be a drain for our team and constantly sharing everything negative. As previously mentioned, we all need to hear positives too. This is about being honest, vulnerable, teachable and supporting each other through messy, real life!

ACTION - Greet an adult or child in the morning, remembering what they previously told you, and watch for a change in demeanour, body language or outlook.

I suggest you watch for changes in the trust and building of a relationship that this brings.

What did you do?	What was the outcome? Didn't work? Try again tomorrow!

We have talked about why we do the job, being vulnerable, teachable, seen, heard, seeing others and the impact of these on ourselves. In writing this I have come to understand that I went through years of school life not stopping to consider why I was always striving to find a better way, be a better version of myself, make more of an impact. I never felt quite good enough nor could I do enough.

I have been on a journey of becoming more self-aware which has indeed led to an increase in seeing that I have value. We looked at self-awareness at the start of this book because it is so key to you discovering and watching for where you make a difference, how you approach situations and how you react. Let's look next at what happens when you learn to believe in yourself!

Chapter 3

Just another cog in the wheel? Do you feel unseen or unappreciated?

Let me tell you a story about when I came back from abroad. I was looking for a part time role. I'd been out of the UK system for a number of years and lacked confidence. I applied for a specialist teacher job. I asked if I could bring my young child as my childcare had fallen through. I pitched up at the interview with a two-and-a-half-year-old and a large bag of distractions (I hoped!). My son did so well until near the end of the interview when we weren't watching him so closely and he quietly wandered out of the room into the next door office. To my consternation this was occupied by the (then) head of Kent Education. I dashed in and quietly but firmly removed the absconder who was happily emptying the contents of the rubbish bin, and we continued the interview. At the end, I was told I would be offered the job on the basis that if I could stay calm in that situation, I could probably be calm in a behavioural support role in schools.

In that moment I realized that I still had something to offer, perhaps more than I realised. Years of experience in different challenging settings abroad had given me skills that perhaps I had underestimated or not recognized or valued. Could this be the same in your case? Have you ever even stopped to think what your skillset is, what you have to offer?

School staff spend their careers supporting children to identify, build then further extend their skills. What about you?

School is a busy place, always will be, whatever we do! Children move, speak, learn, laugh and cry and we go with them! It will always be messy, fun and a little chaotic, even when there is a good structure, leadership, teamwork and support. The problem is that exhausted, burnt-out people are not able to be as effective as those who are valued and "seen", and who know what they bring to their role.

You are a golden cog!

I want you to start this chapter by thinking about what you contribute, who you are and what you have to offer. Simply by being yourself and sharing your gifts, skills, empathy, kindness and courage you will impact the children and your team. When starting to write this book, school staff told me how they felt in their school. The key messages tended to be that they felt unseen, an invisible part of a machine, or that they felt they rarely received affirmation or recognition for their hard work.

As you come to understand the fullness of who you are and what you bring to the messy machine of school life, you become more than an unseen cog, you become a crucial element that helps that machine to work, to tick over, to run!

Did you know that a cog in a machine has the teeth, that when engaged, enable the machine to move? A small part yet so crucial. That is each of us, whatever our role!

I walked through a large primary school one day and this is a list of what I saw:

- A TA chatting to a child, discovering he hadn't had any breakfast
- A TA reading 1:1 with a child, building their self-esteem
- An adult helping a child leave their parent at the school door and get into the building
- A child showing the adult in school a large bruise - maybe important, maybe not
- A TA using gentle questions to check a child had understood the task
- A TA scribing key words onto a white board so the child could remember the task
- An adult gently pushing Maths resources towards a child to encourage them to try the task independently
- An adult helping a child with a nosebleed
- An adult playing catch with a group of children on the playground
- A life-skills group preparing Y6 for transfer to Secondary - a lot of laughter!
- A child making playdough with a safe adult, visibly calming as he mixed it up

I'm sure you could add plenty of things to this list that you see or do through the day. This was a 30 minute snapshot. Do you ever stop to think about the list of achievements, amazing things you accomplish each day?

Who notices that quiet word you gave to the distressed child to enable them to be included? Who notices the hour you spent last night making the resource to ensure that the group could access the session?

I want to remind you that if you work in a school, you have such an immense impact on the children you support. Can you see that? You make them feel safe. You help them to be happy. You encourage them. Motivate them. Coax them. Believe in them. Love them. Laugh with them. Praise them. Affirm them... This is treasure for every child. You open for them a treasure chest of opportunities to grow, become their best, reach their potential, blossom, thrive! What a gift you give them.

We can notice and pick up on positive impact both in ourselves as well as in others. Let's agree to celebrate ourselves and the wins of others! You contribute, whatever your role, to a well-oiled machine of school life!

The real issue we face!

Gallup states that a recent survey on work-related stress and exhaustion reveals that education workers hold the number one and two spots for the most burned-out professionals in the USA.

Responses from a wide range of school staff in both UK and USA has indicated a similar concern around burnout for staff in a range of roles. Colleagues in Australia and France have responded with similar issues.

In the UK, according to research, burnout in teachers comprises three symptoms: emotional exhaustion, depersonalisation, and reduced accomplishment. These symptoms have wide-ranging consequences for teachers.

The studies examined by Madigan and Kim's research show that burnout is associated with lower levels of job satisfaction and worse physical and mental health

It is clear that this is an issue within so many schools, for many levels of staff. Don't discount the headteachers: they feel it, as do teachers, teaching Assistants, office staff. I've seen it myself, experienced it, read about it. We know it's true. Let's agree to take some small steps to make a difference for ourselves and our team.

Time to believe in yourself!

The purpose of this book is to help you to dare to believe more in yourself and see what that does to your self-belief, your daily life. Sounds so simple - well I think it probably is! (Caveat - simple does not equal easy!)

Over the years, I've had the honour of learning from and working with some truly outstanding people and this has had an enormous impact on me. I hope to be able to share some of the things I have learnt from them along the way!

Do you matter?

A little while ago I asked someone I respected greatly whether she could or would advise me on next steps. Where I might be able to develop my skills next. Her reply was simple "Ro, you can do whatever you want!" That stopped me in my tracks. What would you think if someone you respected said that to you? Seriously... what would you think? Who do you REALLY respect?

Who?

Now consider what you would think if they said this to you:

YOU CAN DO WHATEVER YOU WANT!

Take a few minutes and jot down your thoughts. These might be small or big things, but to hope and dream is so important. I question myself constantly. Do my thoughts rob me of confidence? Do I have courage to try something new? You might have an idea for a new project, want to ask for training, have a suggestion that would help your team's daily wellbeing, anything.

Trying something that is your idea, or even a shared idea with others, gives you ownership, drive, energy. Try it. Start small. See if there is impact. Give it time! I felt so frustrated at one point due to lack of funding locally for some of our children. I heard of someone locally who was helping so I organised for him to come to school to chat with me and a small number of staff from other nearby schools. It was great to see the opportunities that arose from this small idea and this experience certainly gave me a moment of energy and enthusiasm for my role. This resulted in a donation to each school for specialist input. Great win, small input!

> **Top Tip** - Dare to have an idea and try it out!

Finding your value starts with…

YOU NEED TO UNDERSTAND WHAT YOU HAVE TO OFFER. You have to recognise this first. Rather than seeing yourself as an unseen cog, I hope you are starting to see that you are a golden cog!

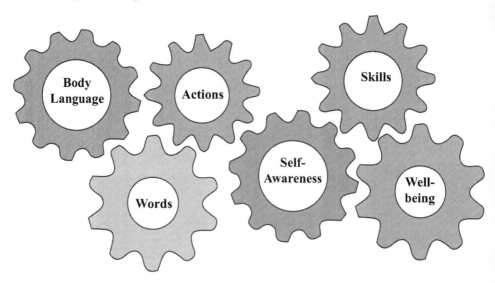

We will revisit this image later as you discover what else you offer to the machine of your school.

This may seem trite, but can I challenge you to notice one small thing each day where you made a difference to someone in school that went unnoticed, yet helped that person's day? This way, even if you feel unseen, undervalued, you start to build your own tank of evidence of your own impact. Quick reminder, remember your body language conveys over 50% of your communication. Watch to see what happens if you adjust this too!

Day	Jot down 1 small thing here that starts to build your evidence bank. Remember- SMALL! Unnoticed by others!
Monday	
Tuesday	
Wednesday	
Thursday	
Friday	

Top Tip - Notice where YOU make a difference

What might flourishing look like?

We all want to flourish. What does this actually mean? Is it simply being seen or affirmed? The dictionaries combine to use words such as grow, thrive, achieve success, prosper. These all sound good to me, and I don't want to settle for less.

I had to have a conversation with a five-year-old recently who had not been listening to his teacher all morning and disrupting the class. I asked him what he had been doing and why. He knew exactly what he had been doing but couldn't tell me why. I told him that he was such a lovely boy, he was so special, naming some of his particular qualities. I told him I believed he could go back into class that afternoon and show his teacher just how special he was. The next day, his mum came to see me and told me that he had gone home and told her he was special. That appeared to be all he heard from our chat! I'd love to say he was an angel from that day on: not quite! But he did start to believe that someone else saw his value and that is a start to him not needing to get attention in other ways.

It's a human need to want affirmation, let's not pretend otherwise. However, how we seek it is crucial. Flourishing is so much more than this. We need to believe in ourselves in order to notice our impact and therefore our successes, wins, moments where we thrive.

I remember making a personalised visual prompt for a child. It took me a while as he was specific with what he wanted on it. I shared it with him, and it improved his self-regulation so much, I wanted to tell everyone. I soon realised, though, that people around me didn't have time to listen, not because they didn't care, but they had too many things to do. A moment to log the win for myself gave me satisfaction, a moment of flow or flourishing.

My hope is that you are starting to understand that rather than being an unseen cog in a huge machine, you are a crucial part of that machine which, dare I suggest, needs you, needs you to be the best version of yourself, needs you to realise what you bring, how valuable you are, all you contribute and what an asset you are. Basically, that without you there, that machine would not function as well.

Do you know? Has anyone told you?

A while back I was chatting with an Executive Headteacher whom I greatly respect. She asked me why I hadn't applied for the job that was on offer, a step up for me. I responded that it hadn't crossed my mind to do so. She asked me why not, then she said words that have stuck with me for about 5 years "Why not? You are good Ro. You know you are good at what you do!" Well, the simple fact was that I DID NOT KNOW THAT, or perhaps hadn't stopped long enough to consider that might be true, or perhaps didn't dare hope this might be a fact.

Because you are starting to notice the impact you are having, you are more likely to realise you are SEEN or NOTICED or VALUED, even if this comes from an unlikely source! You can then start to flow or flourish. You are becoming more self-aware (or were you in the top 15%?) and noticing the impact you have, I hope. What does this have to do with your wellbeing and your self-belief? Turn the page; next is a challenging chapter! At least it was for me!

Chapter 4

Nurturing the Flame. Do you know your strengths? Do others?

"That was crazy! Are they really talking about me? Is that how they see me?" This was the feedback on a staff training session where the eighty or so staff were asked to write on post-it notes what they saw as the main strengths of their colleagues, those they worked closely with. Many were amazed by the qualities colleagues noticed in them. They included kindness, generosity, always stepping in to help.

What do you think others might write about you?

Let's think out of the box for a minute: do you know what makes you flourish? Thrive? Flow? Be your best? Do your best? Mihaly Csikszentmihalyi's theory is that people are much **happier** when they enter a state of "flow". He suggests this is when you are "in the zone", when you are using your skills to the utmost. Can you think of times when you had this sense of flow?

You also need to have a sense of fulfilment to do a good job, but how do you achieve this? We all want the day to feel like it has meaning. We want the children to be the best version of themselves, to reach their potential, right? What about you? What do you bring to the table? Here is the courageous part...

How do your strengths link to your sense of wellbeing?

Don't look ahead. Write down the two or three main strengths that you think you bring to your role. These are your core abilities, what you believe you do well, give yourself two minutes, don't overthink it.

Think of the knowledge, skills, abilities and behaviours that you value the most in what you offer to your role. What are your top three?

1	2	3

Having done this myself, I wrote down that my own most valued strengths were problem solving and capacity to care for and support others. I then took my courage in both hands and asked some of the team I work with what they saw as my key strengths/ skills/ abilities that I brought to my role. Well, I was never so surprised! People responded with decisive, calm in a storm, listener, fun. These were not necessarily what I would have seen in myself.

ACTION - Be brave and go and ask colleagues what they see are your main strengths:

1	2	3
4	5	6

What do you notice? In her book called Flourishing, Maureen Gaffney refers to our "Core Competencies" as those qualities we really value in ourselves. These are your strengths. She explains that in order to be the best version of you, you need to be using your core valued competencies within your role.

Look at your own valued core competencies and those seen by your colleagues.

Are you surprised? Why	
Do they match at all with your own most valued competencies?	

Reflect for a minute: if you are a teacher and what you value most in yourself is that you are a clear communicator, then you will be likely to be thriving as you will use this skill every day! If you are a teaching assistant and you realised you greatly value task completion, you may be getting frustrated. I'm not talking about looking for a new job here, simply seeking ways to use your own valued core competencies.

Do you currently use your valued competencies in your role? When?	

Can you see ways you can ask your team to adjust or add a task to your role to enable you to start using your valued strengths? For example, each day, set yourself one task you will complete, even if all the others go unfinished - seems simple? Try it! We are talking about simple solutions that can make a big difference to your day!

Could you take on something that might enable you to use those skills that you value better? E.g.?	

As a special needs coordinator (SENco) for years, I used to get drained by the feeling that I so rarely completed a task, especially the ones I didn't really like doing. I needed some element of task completion to keep me driven and energetic. For me, I can see this feeds me, it helps me stay on track. It contributes something to my sense of wellbeing.

> **Top Tip** - One job you will complete each day

It was only in very recent years that I understood this and took the helpful advice of trying to start my day with the worst job. That way, my brain is at its best, the children are not in school yet, (fewer distractions) and I start my day with a positive feeling of accomplishment.

> **Top Tip** - Start your day with the worst job!

This is such an easy way to get a win at the start of the day!

One teacher told me that she makes a list of her jobs, then orders them according to urgent, what can wait and what someone might be able to do with her or for her.

A teaching assistant told me that finding a space to store and order her resources helped her to feel she had a small amount of control in her somewhat messy and chaotic day.

A SENco told me that she tidies her desk at the end of each day before going home. In doing this, she starts the next day with some sense of order.

A senior leader told me that they try to make sure they leave five minutes at the end of their day to jot down quietly things to do tomorrow, and reflect on a positive takeaway from their day. They focus on this, then leave slowly, rather than rushing out and remembering all the things they hadn't completed.

Any of these ideas can contribute towards your finding a sense of achievement, satisfaction, accomplishment, control and flow. Maybe jot down something that you have noticed works for you, and try to prioritise it. See what happens.

Top Tip (your own):

Looking at wellbeing from another angle

According to Martin Seligman, wellbeing includes positive emotions, intense engagement, good relationships, meaning and accomplishment.

We all experience highs and lows throughout our day. If you think about each of these components in turn, where do you stand on the wellbeing curve? We often look at where children might be on a curve of wellbeing: how about you?

My curve would look a bit like this right now:

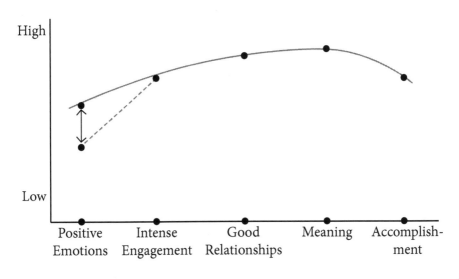

My engagement is high as I write, challenge myself, use my core strengths and values (there is a lot of problem solving and care!). My emotions, however, go up and down daily as I fight feelings of inadequacy about my writing and the impact I had in my past roles. The other areas are pretty good right now.

Now this second curve is me 5 years ago:

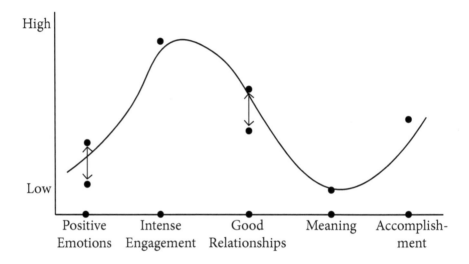

Five years ago, as an assistant headteacher and SENco, my graph would have looked like this, pretty different, I know! On reflection this is likely to be due to my clearly making an impact yet never feeling I could do enough, be enough. Relationships were overall good but just one or two threw out the overall sense of positivity in that area because I was so drained and often felt unseen.

Can you populate on this third graph (opposite page) where you are right now?

Did you know that studies have been done to see why some workplaces are more productive than others? One of the main findings is that when you like coming to work, enjoy your work, this gives you energy and greater impact. We (and I'm sure ALL

OF US) want to be productive, feel we make a difference and make an impact - this all contributes to us being happy in work.

<u>Your own curve:</u>

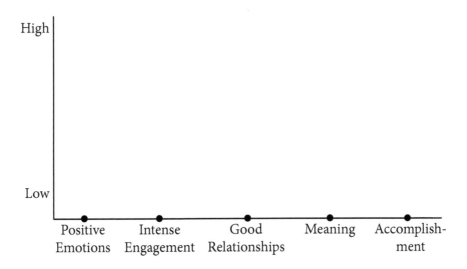

As you start watching for where you get your WINS during your day, where you make a difference, where you use your valued strengths, start to have more confidence in your abilities, decision making, skills and responses, you will then start to gain energy and enjoy work more.

<u>Let's talk about challenge!</u>

Did you know that "owning a challenge" contributes to you thriving?

One year I offered to help turn around a part of a school that required a boost in standards, engagement, fun and organisation. I'd been involved in similar projects before and had a gifted teacher to train and support. We put in a huge amount of energy, enthusiasm and time to the challenge. After three to six months I could see quite clearly that it wasn't working. Staff wellbeing wasn't improving, standards were not transferring across the classrooms, something wasn't right. I had taken on a challenge that was too many steps, or out of my skill set, I'm still not sure. I owned it but was not realistic about my own strengths. I really struggled with feelings of failure and disappointment.

However, a year on and I was asked to oversee behaviour. I worked with and supported another member of staff to make a radical whole school shift in approach. This was an area of passion for me, my strengths matched the skills required (= flourishing), the challenge was perfect for me. It quickly took on shape. In both of these examples, I worked with skilled and enthusiastic colleagues and the results of the challenges were very much to do with my skill set and how many steps of challenge I could manage at that time, alongside whether the skills required matched my skills. Remember - it's OK to win some and lose some!

> **Top Tip** - Note that I found FLOW when the challenges exactly matched my abilities

I don't know about you, when I pursue something that I feel passionate about it energises me, even if I have to squeeze it in between other important things during my week.

We were short of teaching assistants in my school, and I wondered if there was another way we could find energetic, teachable adults to apply. I had an out of the box idea and went for it. This was a new government initiative for apprentice TAs. It did take some time, but because I was excited to see if it might work, I had drive and energy and even a more positive outlook to my day. I should emphasise it worked to a point. Although following my heart with an idea, even a small one, didn't reduce my workload or help the deadlines, it enabled me to encounter a little of what it means to thrive. I saw a bit of flow in my day!

Do you have a project, idea or passion that you would like to pursue? I suggest you start with a small idea and see how it impacts you. I asked at a recent training day if staff had any ideas of things they might like to invest some time in that might enable this. Staff came up with some huge projects and some smaller ones. The point was that they had a sense of ownership, making a difference, trying something new, a challenge they could take on to build hope into their day. The idea of this is not to increase your workload, it is to give you a small project to ponder on that makes you flourish, flow and find energy.

<u>Document the progression of your idea in this box</u>

Give it a week- write how you are doing:

Give it a month - write feedback.
How is it going? How do you feel about your idea?

Learning - we win some and lose some!

If we accept that we are always learning, we can become stronger through the mistakes we make, the disasters that happen and the hiccups that take place along the way. Let me share an example: A few years ago, I was leading a drive to improve attendance. One family had particularly poor attendance, so I was working with them to help the children get into school more regularly. It was working but then attendance dipped after a holiday. After no one answered the phone, I went to the house to see if I could collect the children. I discovered an ambulance at the door called to treat the child who had contracted malaria while abroad. I felt so bad for pushing the family to get into school when they had a valid reason for not being in. Not my best day I admit, but a learning curve that has held me in good stead and helped me improve how I monitor when to follow up and when not to in attendance issues!

I challenge you to believe that unless you dare to try new things, to get things wrong occasionally, and to learn from these things, you are unlikely to get better at what you do and have that sense of believing you can make a difference!

Do you feel like a rag?

I had a dream of a cloth, like a face cloth or cleaning cloth. I tried to wipe something with it. When it was dry, it was completely ineffective. I then wiped a surface with it when it was a little damp and it picked up all the dirt.

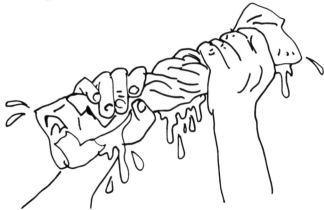

I saw that when it was full of water, not squeezed dry, it didn't absorb the dirt in the same way, and it dripped water instead. Bear with me here - we are NOT talking about cleaning; we are talking about you and your self-worth!

When you feel dried out, you are less effective. When squeezed dry, we pick up rubbish around us, we tend to focus on more negatives. But when full (i.e. feeling valued, energetic and confident) we then can be the best version of ourselves and impact those around us as we work from the overflow of what is inside us. But how do we get to a place where we are working from FULL? What does FULL even mean?

At the beginning of this chapter I mentioned an inset on the wellbeing of staff. Feedback from the morning was that the favourite part was when they each went round telling each other what they saw as that colleague's core strength or what skill they valued in that person - people were so encouraged and sometimes even amazed at how they were perceived, just as I hope you were when you tried this earlier. I wonder what reactions you received? Did others want to share this idea?

Do you know what fills up your cloth? What dries out your cloth? In a school, and probably in the whole of life, we are constantly having demands made on us. We are "giving out".

Drip, drip, drip - can you identify what drains you the most? For me, it was when parents became angry and I had to work hard to bring calm so we could talk about issues constructively. Being a parent of 4 children, I understand our job is to fight for our children, but I have always suggested to parents we can be more impactful if we can work together.

Never getting anything ticked off my to-do list was a drain for me too, whereas each tick off the list was a filler!

When issues cropped up at home for me, I would come into work (as we all do), trying to put on a bold front, needing to just "get through" my day. I'm sure you know the feeling. Life is just like that, right?

I suggest, in a similar way to how you have already identified your strengths, if you can now identify those things that drain you and fill you, you can watch to make sure your day isn't too tipped in a negative direction; you may need to go proactively looking for those things that fill you, on those days that have a will of their own and go in a draining direction!

What fills you up?	What drains you?	Any actions you can take/ask for to re-balance your day?

Let's finish with the 5:1 ratio

We've looked at what drains you and what seems to fill your cloth (your tank). You know a little more of what your main strengths are and when you use these in your role, so I hope you are starting to recognize times of flow in your day, and why.

Going back to Maureen Gaffney, she asserts that research discovered that we will flourish if we have approximately 5:1 positive to negative interactions through our day. If we have less than 3:1 we are in trouble and we lose energy and enthusiasm for our role.

Does this surprise you? I was undecided about whether to put this crucial ratio into the team chapter or here, as it is so linked. You really can't develop this level of flourishing without your colleagues being on board, can you? But you can make a start to tip the balance in the right direction.

Let's take a moment to think about the interactions you have. Remember, home and work mix together in this ratio. If you come into school with a few on the negative side, you may need extra positives to balance the scales!

I had a morning when I woke so early to get myself and my children ready for work and school. One of my teenagers was making a determined effort to persuade me he couldn't go to school that day. We ended up putting a bacon sandwich by the door with a coffee so he could smell them, and he eventually moved!

Exhausting! Two more arguments with children later, and after a hug from my youngest, we were in the car, and I arrived at work a bit later than I'd have liked. Walking through the door, someone held open the door so I could get in with my bags hanging off me, someone else asked if I'd finished the report they needed, another smiled a good morning to me, while another quietly pointed out that my jumper was on back to front without anyone else noticing.

Can you see that within five minutes of being at work, I'd encountered many positive and negative interactions? I expect there were so many more that I probably wouldn't even have logged in the speed of the morning, but does this give you an idea of what I am talking about? Again, as with all the other strategies in this book, the fact that you are noticing, paying attention, simply means you can then do something about it. Log the positive intentionally - that makes them more powerful. Watch for them! Look at the first couple of hours or last couple of hours in your school day, even lunch time; can you spot if your interactions are in a positively balanced ratio?

In the next chapter we will look at the team you work with. If you have made it this far you have already been considering the interactions you have with your team. The relationships, trust, the support you give and receive, all contribute to your own sense of self belief and potential to thrive. You can rarely choose your team, so let's look at strategies that might help you to thrive more within that team, to find the best version of you so both you and your team benefit. Surely this can only be a win-win situation?

One positive interaction	One negative interaction	Impact on you

Balance at the end of the day	Ratio:	How do you feel?
One action step for tomorrow to redress the balance?		

Chapter 5

Collaboration, productivity and relationships. Are you in an effective team?

When I lived in Poland in the early 1990s, I helped to set up an international school which was on a very tight budget. When it became very cold in the winter, the heating wasn't efficient enough so I would take my class outside, well wrapped up, and stomp around in the playground singing army mantras about how we might be cold but we wouldn't freeze. Knowing I'm not great in the cold, colleagues would come and take over from me, so that I could go and teach in one of their warmer classrooms for a while. We had so much fun - I ended up teaching GCSE Maths, English as an additional language, music and phonics all in one day. This was possibly one of the most effective teams I have worked with over the years. Why? I think it was largely because we were all honest and vulnerable with each other, seeing the benefits of using each other's strengths for the good of the whole team.

<u>What is the best team you have ever worked in?</u>

Can you think for a moment? What about the team you work in now? Do you feel you belong? Do you have trusted relationships, support when you need it, and are you asked for help when others need it? Do you feel seen? Appreciated? Are your skills used? Why does this matter?

Answer these questions - then think about how you feel right now. This is a starting place from which to launch yourself into a better place. Take 2 minutes - don't overthink it. We will discuss this more in a minute. This is your gut reaction.

What do you think might make up a great team?

Think about your current team.
Are your responses different? Why?

Even in the most effective teams every day will bring its own set of challenges. With this in mind, we need to be aware of our own emotional state and also aware of those around us. Maureen Gaffney in her book on Flourishing puts it this way:

"When you are internally attuned, it is easier to be attuned to others and you engage with them in a more effective and creative way."

I certainly want to engage with my team in this way, so it seems worth the investment to become more aware of ourselves, our emotional state, words, thoughts and actions.

I worked with a headteacher once who tended to be absorbed with himself and his family, his own needs. He would ask us how we were but not really listen or support. He would bring the conversation back to himself. He lacked self-awareness and was not attuned to himself or those around him. Can you identify with this? Are you prepared to consider that this may ring a little true for yourself or watch for it in those around you? I know that when I am really struggling myself, I am less self-aware, so I have to make a bigger effort to make sure I am watching for how those around me are doing.

Let's build your TEAM jigsaw

During my time working in schools, only twice have I worked closely with one other person to complete my job, it was like having a job share. Reflecting on why each of these opportunities to work closely with a colleague was both more fun and more effective, I would say that the year I had a special needs coordinator (SENco) work alongside me, although she was younger and less experienced, she was faster than me and found more effective ways of doing things.

Then I worked as Inclusion lead, with the Wellbeing lead sitting beside me and for a year we brought wellbeing to the front of the agenda for the school. Again, this was a pleasure, perhaps because our conversations always started with "How are you (honestly)?" and "Can I help with anything?" Perhaps because we were both so passionate about the outcome, we spurred each other on, the challenge was set, and we responded by dividing our skills (hers being much greater than mine!).

The overall theme of these "teams" was that we were all teachable, willing to learn from each other, accepting that our opinion would be heard but could also be changed, so we attuned to each other. If you look at this team jigsaw-puzzle, what comes to your mind? What qualities make up those in your team right now? What makes a difference? What helps or doesn't?

In this jigsaw, write down the qualities you see in your team at the moment. Consider your own emotional state alongside that of your colleagues as you fill in the pieces:

Now let's consider the most effective team you have been involved with, seen or read about. What qualities might you put into this jigsaw such as self-awareness or attunement?

Compare your current team jigsaw to that of a healthy, well performing team. What are the differences, if any?

Each person in your school is a crucial piece of the jigsaw to ensure you have a powerful team to bring maximum impact to your children and their families. At the same time, each of you is also a valued and important team member, and therefore every single member of your team matters.

How do you fit in? How do you feel about your team? Take a moment…

In my experience in schools, we tend to be quick to ask senior leaders to make changes to make a difference for our team, the dynamics, the ethos, leadership, resources, time etc. I want to suggest that as a team member, **you** can also decide today to ask yourself the question:

"What could *I* do to make a difference to my team?"

When I put this to a group of staff members I had been working with, they could all come up with things I could do but struggled to think of things each of them could do!

How can you become a better TEAM member?

Let's have a quick look at two models that help us when working within an effective team. I have chosen these two purely because I have used them myself in schools and seen the impact that highlighting them has had.

The first is the Window of Tolerance:

When in our Window of Tolerance, as described originally by Dan Siegal, we are at our most effective level of functioning, and are most able to respond to the demands of our day. This is where you can maintain emotional regulation, you can think clearly, and function effectively. You are likely to be familiar with this model, so let's dig in a little and identify what helps you to stay within this healthy space.

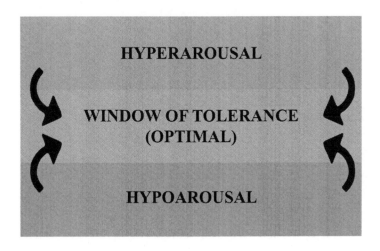

After coming across this model years back, I started to watch for when I might be moving out of my Window of Tolerance. The signs for me were a racing heartbeat, buzzing in my head, wanting to walk away, or starting to feel anger. I also noticed that just by watching for these changes within myself, I could take a moment, an extra breath, give myself a quick talking to; in order to come back into my optimal Window. I have also noticed that when I move into the lethargic space and become unmotivated, I have had to learn strategies such as taking a walk to bring myself back into my Window of Tolerance.

We all know that our mood goes up and down through each day, but during these swings, we want to stay within our Window of Tolerance. Wonderfully, simply by being aware of this emotional regulation tool, we can start to train ourselves to increase our awareness of where we are within the window and whether we are slipping out of our Window of Tolerance.

You can't necessarily avoid certain situations where you get anxious or perhaps lethargic, but you can learn strategies that help you to watch for when you are slipping out of your Window of Tolerance, and so learn to pull yourself back in!

	Name a time in the last week when you were in this box	What were your feelings/symptoms in this space?	How can you get back into your optimal window?
HYPER-AROUSAL			
WINDOW OF TOLERANCE			
HYPO-AROUSAL			

Vulnerability, teachability, or both to improve your TEAM?

Johari's window is a well-known model and helps us increase our self-awareness, leading to better connection within our team and improved authenticity. Do you know what makes you tick? It was developed by Luft and Ingham in the 1950's and it is still seen to be important.

	Known to self	Not known to self
Known to others	**Open Area** (1)	**Blind Spot** (3)
Not known to others	**Hidden** (2)	**Unknown** (4)

The crucial thing for this journey of discovering your value is to understand that none of these windows is a set size. They can each expand and shrink as you move down this road. What is in each window for you? Keep your team in mind. In the first window you will all know certain things about you. Everyone who knows me well knows that I love a challenge, I'm a teacher, a Christian, have four children and I am willing to communicate this publicly.

The second window is the masked or hidden window. This includes those things I am keeping private from you, like my fears, some of my dreams. This can change over time. Through this book

I have revealed that I have had times where I have felt inadequate and what I have done about it. This means window 2 shrinks and window 1 grows. As I have shared this, I have become empowered and feel stronger as a result of sharing it. Do you have something once hidden that you now talk about openly?

The third window contains things about you, positive or negative, that you don't know about, but others do. The key here, is that if you are open to feedback from friends or colleagues you can grow. For example, I was told once that I was finishing the sentences of a colleague on a regular basis. Just becoming aware of this and accepting the feedback helped me to change, hopefully mature and become a less annoying team member or person to work with!

The fourth window (unknown to both you and others) is where you have the opportunity to experiment, try new things that you don't yet know about, so you end up discovering more about yourself. You don't know if you will be good at, or like these things. Are you willing to have a go? This could reveal or teach you new things about yourself. The first time it was suggested to me that I try making a YouTube video to share some of my journey, I flatly refused. I'm an introvert at heart and the thought of it sent my heart pounding. However, when I tried, I discovered it was so much fun. It gave me a buzz and it even helped some others, which increased the feel of flow that I received.

For the brave!

Can you think of an area where you have self-doubt, feel inadequate, or simply an awareness that you have a lack of skills. Perhaps you'd like to try something new? Be trained in a new area or simply stretch yourself? Can you then ask for help with this? Even small areas where we lack skills, when addressed, can have a huge impact on our wellbeing, energy, effectiveness and outlook.

I worked with an amazing TA who often spoke of her concerns about using the white board when covering classes. After a while, she received training for this which enabled her to become a more effective and useful team member. However, most importantly, she stopped worrying about it! Which windows might expand or shrink in this case?

Perhaps you could go a step further and ask a trusted colleague for feedback on one small thing that might make you a better team member? Remember that by adjusting how we go about our day, as we make positive changes this can result in a greater impact both on your level of flow or flourishing, but also on your team.

> Write here your idea which would
> involve you taking brave action:

At an interview for a job, I had to take an assembly. I was concerned about this as I hadn't even sat in an assembly for years due to the nature of my role. In the feedback from the interview and observation, I was offered the job but they explained that the weak area had been my assembly. I felt so inadequate, and it became a huge worry for me, like a grey cloud over my head. However, I taught myself, thanks to videos on the internet, and soon became competent – I even enjoyed them! I remember a colleague recently watching one of my assemblies and commenting that I appeared to be in my happy place during these sessions. Crazy as it may seem, something that started as an incompetence became a place of flow and flourishing for me.

In Chapter 3, when talking about challenge, I explained that in trying to move on a set of classes with a colleague, I had to confront my lack of skill and abilities I thought I had but I did not have. In this situation, I could possibly have learnt what was needed, but I agreed with my headteacher that my skills were better used elsewhere. This was hard for me to accept as failure didn't sit well with me. Looking back, however, I see this as a learning opportunity: that we can't all be good at everything. Perhaps that glass of opportunity needed to be handed on to someone else?

Remember your jigsaw of your team? I bet you don't all have the same set of skills!

What do you bring to your team?

At this point, have you thought of additional aspects to a well-functioning team above? Check out your jigsaw.
If you google what makes a successful team, the most common words appear to be communication, collaboration and honesty. Can you see a theme here? Remember my team in Poland at the start of this chapter? These are what made it work so effectively.

- Trust
- Loyalty
- Relationship
- Vulnerability
- Teachability
- Honesty
- Safety
- Tolerance

- Energy
- Enthusiasm
- Listening
- Investment
- Creativity
- Hard work
- Patience
- Laughter

- Purpose
- Communication
- Kindness
- Collaboration
- Shared purpose
- Self-awareness

Now can you tick which of these qualities you have seen within your team.

Go back to thinking about what you bring. Is there an area you could develop in yourself to support your team?

Remember you can't expect to have all the skills others have, but working together collaboratively we can share skills. Next, we will look at how this feeds into helping with workload and managing your time. You may have skipped straight to Chapter 6 as this tends to be such a major barrier for school staff, but I'm hoping the buildup works together as a package deal. Each element builds to help the others. Let's see...

Chapter 6

How good are your juggling skills?

I once read a SENco's (special needs coordinator) Facebook feed on how they arrived at work in reasonable time and left promptly every day. They had clear boundaries, got everything done and suggested we should all be able to do the same. I can't describe how angry, frustrated, mad, jealous, and generally upset I felt. I suppose there was a little part of me that thought that they must have a magic formula and had it all sorted. Perhaps they were more proficient and skilled at the job than me? I felt ineffective, inefficient and inadequate; all in all I felt that I must be doing something wrong. I was in the same role yet I was arriving early and leaving late alongside working many hours at home simply to survive.

How does that comment make you feel?

When I came to reflect on these feelings of frustration, I realised that through my day, I so often feel that way anyway. In school, every day, we hit scenarios that we have never encountered before, hear things we have never heard, see things that amaze and astound us, frighten and challenge us. When we try something that doesn't work - how do we react? We say something that comes out wrong, what do we do? We are always rushing and therefore do not always give a task the time needed due to the juggle of the school day. I bet the ones you remember at the end of the day are the ones that went wrong! We have to react fast, and overall, we do this so well! So many times each day we get things right.

Your glass

A friend told me that he doesn't see a glass as half full or half empty, but he looks at that glass and wonders what opportunity it presents to him. For him it is an opportunity to make a difference.

Let's look at the school day for staff. Whether class teachers, teaching assistants, special needs coordinators or leaders, the focus is on meeting the needs of the children, bringing out their potential, overcoming barriers and engaging them (all of them) with all their varying needs. The bureaucracy and workload required to enable this is now huge. I remember a day when an office colleague completed an urgent referral, went to unblock a toilet, sat with a distressed child while waiting for a parent to collect him, unjammed a photocopier - then she wiped some dinner tables and finally sat down to eat her breakfast at two o'clock and start her paperwork for the day. Normal school day? Did anyone see, notice, affirm her in these tasks? Many of these things will not have been in her job description but she cared enough to do them anyway. Her glass was an opportunity; she smiled and laughed (and groaned) through the tasks. She saw solutions and needs and stepped in.

The question here is: what do we value? What does your school value? What do you value?

These may seem like obvious questions, but are they? A colleague told me that while teaching he always felt inadequate as he could never quite produce enough paperwork or complete it well enough. Overall, he did not feel valued. However, once he retired, he could see the impact he had on his students. Then he could see more clearly the value of what he had offered and the value of who he was.

Please don't misunderstand me. I'm not blaming leaders here. I was a leader myself for a long time and however amazing the outlook of the school and its ethos is, the expectations on schools are heavy.

In the face of these pressures, are you holding to your values, your ethos and your core beliefs? I worked in a school (only for a short time) where decisions were made that didn't sit well with me. The best way I can describe it, is that I was being asked to drive at 32 miles an hour in a 30 mph limit. I had to stop to reflect to be able to realise this though. I was working such long hours, at such a fast rate, making a really great impact on the children. However, I needed to pause and consider what I could do and what my options were in order to address the issue (remember the "what" and not "why" of self-awareness in Chapter 1?). Once I did this, I was liberated to be me.

Holding onto your values is so important. This also applies when you are asked to do something that you aren't either trained or resourced to do. You may require a certain amount of confidence to stand up for yourself: not in a confrontational way, I hope, but to be able to explain why that task doesn't fit your skills or experience. In order to have the courage to do this, you need to understand your value, but you may not yet have the required skills, that's OK! Remember, small steps!

A teaching assistant came to me to explain that she didn't feel an intervention was making an impact on the children. She was quite stressed about it, behaviour wasn't great during these sessions and it was upsetting both her and the children's day. We looked into it together and discovered that she hadn't had training in this. Easy win! Once trained, she was amazing! The children loved it too and benefitted greatly. How often in school do we try to do things we are not actually equipped to do, probably just to help out (or maybe because you are a people-pleaser like me?).

How long is your TO-DO list?

OK, so let's look at that to-do list. We all have one and all too easily it can become overwhelming.

Be honest with yourself. What are your top five jobs at the moment? I'm talking about the top five things you really need to do. These could be easy things, or perhaps things you've been putting off. Big or small, top five only! Add them to the list on the previous page.

If you look at them as the glass of opportunity, can you turn the tasks on their heads and see a solution to getting them done? Perhaps a reality check moment here would help. I'm not pretending everything will suddenly make you flourish with this action. That pediatric referral you make knowing it will take three years to come to fruition will still be frustrating. Not everything brings instant rewards. Sometimes knowing the reason for completing a task can help though. I worked with a very hardworking TA once who always put off filling in her intervention tracking sheet. I knew these groups were so effective because I'd seen them, and the children as well as the data proved it. I explained to her that her evidence on the tracking sheets enabled me to apply for increased funding for that child. Immediately, there was a purpose for the task and it became easier for her. Dare I suggest that though not loving the task, there was a moment of flow as she knew she was contributing to an end goal for that child and the team. It gave her motivation.

- Are these jobs achievable in the timeframe required?

- Do they even matter?

- Should they be on there?

- Do you know WHY you have to do them?

Simon Sinek suggests that leaders can inspire action within their teams by sharing WHY new initiatives or tasks are being requested. He says this brings motivation, engagement, and loyalty. The reality in school is that we can't always know the reason WHY we have to do things. However, there is great value in knowing WHY when possible.

This book is about you though. I've tried telling staff WHY and this certainly helps. Perhaps the leaders reading this could take this on board. But for those reading this in other roles, how can you take ownership of this yourself? I suggest that you go back to remembering WHY you are doing this job and remind yourself of your skills and strengths. Then make sure you use your core competencies or valued strengths regularly, and this will be a step in the right direction - a step towards greater fulfilment.

That glass, is it tipping over?

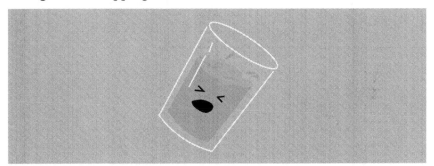

A staff member recently told me they were running on fumes. Home life and school life combined was so much to manage. Sometimes, it is too much and we need to recognise this and go to seek support. However, that glass is also an opportunity. A side point here is to recognize that in asking for help, you may in fact validate and encourage a colleague. I loved it when a colleague came to me to ask for support with a task. It made me feel useful, gave me a sense of flow and certainly energy.

See that glass of water as a glass of your favourite treat drink. Perhaps that wine or glass of juice has more potential than you thought?

Top Tip - Full, empty or opportunity?

Let's go back to your To Do list.

	What could you action today?	What could you action in the next few days?
Can you see any solutions?		
What is important?		
What is most urgent?		
Can you re-order it?		
Could you complete just one item that might then reduce your stress levels?		
Could you speak to someone to get clarity as to WHY?		
Could a large task be broken down into smaller chunks? More manageable steps?		
If you asked for help with one, might it empower the other person? (Do you dare to appear imperfect?)		

Look at your week

I know a gifted teacher who worked extremely long hours. We had a look together at what was taking so much time. We quickly realised they were creating the most beautiful resources for their team and other things were dropping along the wayside. Are you aware of how you prioritise your time? Do you chat for too long at times when you could be planning with the team? Do you create such masterpieces that mean other, more important things get squeezed out? Perhaps filling in that intervention tracking grid has taken a back seat as you don't see it as impacting your group of children? The problem is that you then keep remembering that it might be asked for or needed to track progress, so it hangs over you as a stress. My suggestion is JUST DO IT! It always surprises me how little time these things tend to take. You know those ones we put off? Once we sit and complete them the stress disappears! Are you asking how on earth you can fit in that task? Are you thinking I've forgotten how tight time is in school? I do know, I promise you! But I really hope you are in a team where you can say to a colleague that you need 10 minutes to complete a task, to ask if they might cover you, or help in some way. Perhaps you could ask a colleague to help you complete something together. Make it happen, book it in and protect that time - you will feel better.

You might be really shocked if you break down your week to see what you actually do. It's a bit painstaking for that week but can be quite revealing!

Before School	Before Break	Break	After Break	Lunch	After-noon	After School	Evening

Is there anything that jumps out to you from this analysis?

When I did this, I noticed that I was least effective between 1.30pm and 2.30pm. This was when I moved into the hypoarousal part of my Window of Tolerance. It was easy for me to address this. I simply set up meetings, observations or a proactive task during that time each day so that I wasn't sitting lethargically at my desk.

What could happen if you start to believe in yourself?

We need to talk about boundaries. I do not profess to be an expert. However, as you discover your value, start to believe in yourself and in what you contribute, you will become conscious that being totally wrung out is NOT OK. Can you take a few minutes to consider:

- What matters to you?
- What makes a difference to you?
- What things fill your bucket?
- What things drain you?
- What might you be able to put in place to tip the balance in a healthier direction?
- Remember - one small thing can give you a sense of feeling you have some control, autonomy, peace (take small steps!)

I asked this question to a group of TAs. They all agreed that one thing that gave their day greater purpose and therefore satisfaction, was when they had time to talk to the class teacher, so that when they are being asked to do x or y, they saw the bigger picture. Perhaps this is as simple as being shown the marking from last night and hence the focus for the lesson that day.

Top Tip- Class teacher and TA have regular time to talk

I have tried for years, in different schools, to set up ways for teachers and TAs to meet regularly, because research reports the benefits, and so do staff I've worked with when they made it happen! The thing that has worked in my experience is for each team to make or prioritise a way that works for them. I would suggest this is worth the investment if at all possible.

I walked into a school where one TA had worked as a 1:1 support for a non-verbal child for 2 years. The adult was exhausted, truly on her knees, yet single-mindedly keeping going as she was determined to do all she could for that child. We spent a little time together and talked through her day. She spent so much time on her own, using her own resources, ideas and energy. As soon as we started taking tiny steps to change this, her outlook improved. We started a daily five minute session where she shared the sensory room with another adult and child, therefore reducing her sense of isolation. Such a small step but it brought hope to her day. Perhaps she felt "seen"?

I've worked with a wonderful middle leader who was very skilled, yet at the same time she had such humility, alongside boundaries. This is a rare combination of skills in my experience. She was not afraid to ask for help, knew her limitations and yet this was not seen as a weakness. She appeared to have such confidence in herself. How did she manage it? How does this link to our value? Where is her self-belief from? If her lesson didn't work, she would laugh about it and say she would make adjustments and improve it for tomorrow. She certainly had self-awareness in that her language was asking "What can I do better?" rather than "Why did that go wrong?" Her view of her glass was always that hunt for solutions and opportunities. Every child and team member had something to offer and she built her team around trust, giving each person a voice and then expecting each one to work together to bring the best out in themselves and each other. She was working within her "core competencies", she was not afraid to ask for help and the value she placed on communication and contributions from her team was very evident. Dare I suggest that the value she placed on each of her team then empowered her, enabled her to flourish and flow?

Working in school will always be hard work. The question is whether we can somehow keep it manageable, stay healthy and have some level of balance and satisfaction, even enjoyment. My hope is that in reading this chapter, your awareness of your thoughts, words, expectations and actions enable you to grab a level of control in some area. As you start to notice increasingly the impact and difference you make, you will see the treasure you share with the children and your team. Are you starting to see your value?

This time you are taking to focus on yourself is NOT selfish - let's look at why.

Chapter 7

Balancing it all together.

It was the end of a long week. I'd worked eleven-hour days all week and rushed home to get my children ready to go on a trip. I was late, stressed and tired. We were all running round throwing clothes into bags, hunting for lost socks and shoes when I was reminded that I'd said I would cut all my children's hair. Feeling a rising surge of panic, I grabbed the clippers, plugged them in and shouted for the first child to sit. I marched over to start cutting and decided the fastest route was to start in the middle of the forehead and work back. So I did. Unfortunately, in my rush, I forgot to add the number 4 attachment! You can probably imagine the shrieks, moans and general agony that ensued as I realized I'd shaved a bald line straight down the middle of my child's hair!

Looking after yourself, taking stock of how you are doing, becoming more self-aware and discovering what makes you flow or flourish is NOT selfish. It is good for you, your home life and also for your team at school. I would go as far as to suggest that it is selfish NOT to take some of these steps in order to become the best possible version of you.

Experience has shown me that as a staff member, with "stuff" going on at home constantly, if I'm not OK, this impacts those around me. Investment in yourself does not mean you are wrapped up in yourself or self-centered, but it does empower you, and those you meet. As a parent I know I have made so many mistakes, yet my children have turned out to be amazing. As a SENco, I was always overloaded, yet I can see I had a positive impact on the lives of so many children and families (not always acknowledged, but that's OK, it's not why we do it!). As a deputy headteacher, I put procedures, policies and practices in place that sometimes worked and sometimes didn't - you can't win them all, right? The key for me has been to be teachable and vulnerable (and humble), together with a little self-belief and positive friends and family to support me. I learn something new every day. If we can retain this attitude of readiness to learn, we can master new things. I am certainly imperfect, and many times have needed help (and perhaps should have asked for it!). Sometimes I got it, sometimes I couldn't get it and the struggle was even bigger.

Your value quotient
Where are you right now?

Talking to yourself and others

Can I challenge you on one more thing? How positive or negative is your talk with colleagues? I've worked with RADIATORS (people who encourage, build up and are positive) and DRAINS (those who tend to leave you exhausted, are always telling you about themselves and their problems). Which are you? Remembering that in fact only about 15% of us have a good level of self-awareness, can you watch how you speak over the next week? Do you need to change your talk? Try it. Can you see any impact? Do people react differently? Do you feel better?

What is your internal self-talk like? If you are like me, you have a battle constantly with your self-talk. Regularly I felt that I was not good enough. What has changed my work outlook and self-talk has been a focus on supporting others around me. Does this sound simple? Good, I hope it does! It is. Try it!

> **Top Tip** - Watch the self-talk.
> Point out positives for those around you.

I worked with a leader, who, when I asked if I was doing things as they wanted, responded that I should not need affirmation in this way; it was a weakness (they may not have put it quite so bluntly, but that was my summary to myself!). I quickly realised that I needed to find affirmation, and perhaps self-belief from other sources. So, I started looking for and enjoying lovely things going on around the school, perhaps a teacher affirming a vulnerable child, or a TA bringing out the best in a child or pointing out something amazing that happened in an assembly. Whatever our role, our age, our experience, we all need to be SEEN and recognized, as this builds our self-belief. I started to notice that in affirming others, I felt better about myself.

Whatever your role, could you once a day notice something enabling, positive or caring that someone around you does or says (and speak it out!)? They might start to do it for you. Imagine what that might look like? An even quicker win is to notice something you do that helps a child, a colleague, or a parent. Recognise it, internalise it and notice the impact you have! Feel a moment of flow and self-belief knowing you have made an impact.

If you are feeling more positive about what you have accomplished, about yourself and about the outlook to your day, you will have more energy and enthusiasm - this will result in greater productivity and enjoyment.

Why was it such a battle to believe in yourself? How is your self-worth right now? Do you believe in yourself, see your skills and your successes? Does this make you feel uncomfortable? These are questions for the brave! This is a challenge to be real. You are worth it! Invest in yourself and confront your inner voice. Dare to be bold and write the real response, if not in this space, find a piece of paper. Why? Remember Dr Chapman in the Introduction? He encourages writing things down, so we see them again, we revisit them. In a similar way to journalling. We regularly suggest to children that they journal their thoughts, feelings and ideas as research shows the benefits. I do this, so why not start having a go?

Remember why you came into education? You have so much capacity to grow and empower children as you share with them. Remember your qualities, your love of sharing information, getting excited about children discovering new knowledge, learning new skills and developing the confidence to approach tasks.

Who you are is so important! Not just what you do. Remember the child who smiles at you when they come through the door, just because you are a safe adult to them? Or the older child who comes and tells you they have been journaling as you discussed, and this has helped them so much to stay calmer when they start to become anxious. It could be as simple as you giving an idea for a solution to a colleague who reports back to you that it helped them - smiling at you in relief! That was you sharing your quality time to develop skills, safety, confidence, resilience... What a gift! These small moments can be overlooked in a day of crazy running, juggling, deadlines and demands. Don't let them slip by!

Let's quickly see off a giant!

I knew I needed to speak to the tax man. I'd known for weeks. I'd been putting it off and off. I was dreading the queue to wait to speak to someone, and anyway, when could I find the space in term time to get onto a call like that? I seized the day and made the call at 4.30pm one Friday before I left work. I was put through to a human after only 10 minutes and five minutes later the issue was resolved. I'd had a black cloud over my mind for 3 weeks, dreading a task that in reality was not so huge.

Do you resonate with this at all? If you are anything like me, you will worry about this one job, task, intervention, training, conversation, email, way too much, until it overwhelms your thoughts. Have you ever had a phone call you need to make that seems to hover over you all day? You finally pluck up the energy to make the call and it's over quickly and wasn't as bad as you thought? What about the classroom task that feels way too big and you don't have the energy or time for? From your perspective it is not high priority, for another it is. How about the paperwork task that you have been putting off and putting off that really needs doing.

Top Tip - Just do it!

Putting it off will not help you be your best through the rest of the day and it denies you the focus and energy you so badly need! We all know that feeling overwhelmed effects your sleep and mood. Try putting things on a list so you don't have to keep them in your head. You could even try to keep a certain time each day or week to get these things done.

The Giant in front of you: a task that makes you feel overloaded/ stressed	The Giant in front of you: What might you do? What can you try? (Ask for help, training, resources, etc.?)	What is the impact? Did it help? If not, try another solution

You might want to ask a trusted colleague or friend to help you come up with solutions. Remember - **what is obvious (or difficult) to another is not always obvious (or difficult) to you!**

A story of hope:

A few years ago, I was special needs coordinator in quite a tough school. A group of boys were causing constant disruption in class and the teacher was asking for help. She had tried everything. We discovered the boys were all fixated with football, so I started running a club each week. We scrutinised the newspapers to look at football scores. Unbeknownst to these children, they were analysing data, making predictions, collating, evaluating, discussing, collaborating and perhaps most importantly, getting excited about learning. What I mainly remember from these sessions was the excitement in the boys and their engagement. I had such a feeling of satisfaction; the teacher would chat with the boys daily about upcoming matches and possible outcomes ensuring the boys were "seen" each day and felt valued, and so did the teacher. It took us to put our heads together to come up with a solution.

How about finding a little autonomy?

We all love and need affirmation, and it is motivating to be seen doing effective things that deserve recognition. However, the reality is that most of what we do will not be noticed for different reasons. We do it because we are there for the children and we want to give it our best shot. Right? So, if what we do goes unnoticed, YOU need to take notice instead. I've said it before, watch for the wins! Perhaps start watching for the wins of those around you too and affirming them. You will feel the joy instantly. We all have a need to be able to direct something in our lives. When we feel everything is out of control, we will not be our best version of ourselves. If you can find some autonomy, perhaps a little self-direction, independence or control over even one area at work, this will help you to thrive.

Let's think about this in practice:

You are a teaching assistant, and your day is full of reactionary tasks as well as planned activities and bits and bobs in between. How can you find some order, control and even some sense that what you do matters, to give you some ownership? I worked with an outstanding TA who would take on an intervention across a year group and run it herself. It was so effective there were lists of children waiting to take part. It had huge impact. She would buzz about it, as would the children and the teachers, and she worked hard to prepare it too. At one point I saw that the sessions available had been cut and it had been almost side-lined (not anyone's fault), but the result for her was a sense of disempowerment - she felt de-valued. Why? She had invested so much, and it was taken away which made no sense when we all knew it had such an impact. We had a discussion to share why this needed to be adjusted, recognizing her frustration, and made a plan to re-run the group the following term. For her, this brought her some sense of order again, being seen and heard.

A class teacher had so many children with emotional needs in his class that he was missing all his lunchtimes trying to sort out issues. I watched as he trialled standing by his door each morning and greeting each child, with a short check in. His day drastically changed with a small amount of control and creative thinking as the children responded to being seen, valued and understood. We are not necessarily talking about huge changes we need to make to get quantifiable results.

After a few years as a SENco, I was drowning in paperwork and a SENco in a nearby school told me how she worked from home one day a week to manage this. I asked to try this idea at my school and it transformed my workload, my outlook and my sense of achievement. It wasn't always possible but was a huge help when it did.

I learnt from a senior colleague that in order to get things done, diarising to meet with people to discuss tasks or evaluate them after completion was a very effective way of ensuring they got done. It was also supportive and productive to both people. This gave everyone a sense of autonomy but also of being valued as time was invested in them, rather than the reactionary passing in the corridor and comment asking if that task is finished.

Can you think of an area over which you can take some control?

Area	How?	Impact

Imagine you can say to yourself:

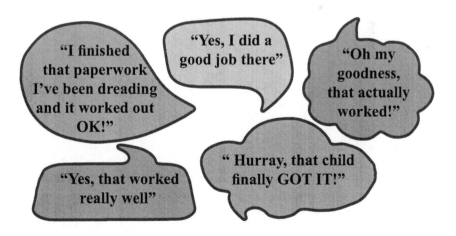

As you notice your own achievements, you become seen and discover your value. On top of this, as you increasingly believe in yourself and the impact you have, you model it to those around you, children and colleagues, the increased value you have. The third outcome is that your team benefits. They see your energy and enthusiasm, your flow and they will almost certainly want some of that!

The balance board

What if you feel overloaded? How can you stay upright? Can you identify what might be tipping you right now? What is one small thing you could do to redress the balance? Remember that even a small thing can have a bigger impact.

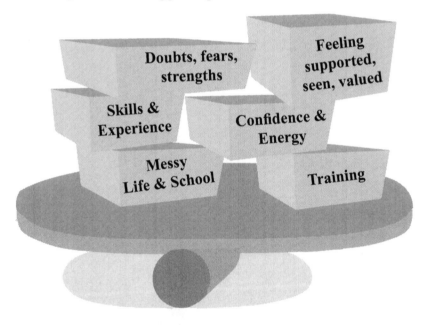

Top Tip - small steps can make a big difference!

At one point, I had my four children in four different schools. School runs were a challenge while trying to get into work at a decent time. In addition to this, I was having a tricky time with my line manager who was putting me down a lot which knocked my confidence. I was supporting some children with needs I hadn't encountered before and was having difficulty accessing sufficient support for them. I was also struggling to see where I was making much impact, as there were no systems set up in the school for feedback that I could find. It was a constant juggle of time, emotions, determination and searching for self-belief. Was I doing a good job? One day, I had a meeting with a very distressed mother of six children who's eldest was getting home from school and running wild, hyper and unable to calm. I remember suggesting she try rolling a gym ball up and down his back as he lay on his tummy straight away on getting through the door. It sounds so simple, but she came back the next week, looking visibly younger, happier and reporting back that it was working. I immediately felt better about myself: I'd made a difference to a family, something I did had worked. I started to experience the feeling of thriving. Of course, I then started to see other things I'd been doing that had been working! I needed my eyes opening, that's all!

Teachability and Imperfection!

You will have setbacks and knocks - we all do, it's part of life, but it does not have to define you! The important bit is what you choose to do when it happens. When my eldest was about 7 years old, I had to pull him out of a school where he was being bullied. I thought I could home school him while we found a better school. Well, I could NOT. I thought that as a teacher, I would be great at this. He certainly didn't think so and we lurched from one failed day to another: refusals, tears (from both of us!), paper thrown around, tantrums and more refusals. The more creative I became, the worse things got. I tried every strategy that has ever worked on my toughest classes - nothing worked. So I gave in and we quickly found him a school. What a steep learning curve for me!

My skills as a class teacher did not transfer to my son. I have such respect now for parents who manage this. Congratulations! Why did it go wrong? Wrong question! Instead, what for us was a solution to this problem? What could I do about it? Not mixing the parent/teacher role, we couldn't manage this, so find a school! We won't all be good at everything. The question is, are you willing to accept this? There are some things we can learn to do or to get better at (and you may have to do this in your role) but others you should admit to not being your forte and let another person do it. They may flourish in that task or role.

In summary

Remember the feeling of being an unseen cog in a wheel, or machine, invisible and unvalued? Let's revisit what you bring to the messy machine of school life, just to embed the image in your mind.

I hope you have found some strategies that have helped you, that you have tried and that have positively impacted you and your team. Perhaps relationships have improved, you have more energy or there are moments where you have experienced flow. Have you started to understand better the value you carry?

Can you start to see your wellbeing from the perspective of your core value rather than your productivity? The irony is that as you do this, your productivity (and that of your team) is likely to grow!

> **Top Tip** - Believe in yourself

Hopefully you have come to see that as you invest in yourself, believe in yourself and use your key strengths alongside becoming more self-aware, there are benefits. These are both for you, your efficiency, your enjoyment and outlook, but also for those around you.

Have you recognised times in your day where you flow, thrive or flourish, even for short periods of time? I have used these words interchangeably throughout the book because we each identify with these terms in our own way in our own time. What matters is that you can start to watch for those moments when you achieve this positive state of being.

I hope that you have come to see that you are worth investing in! We are all conscious of our weaknesses and tempted to self-doubt. However, I challenge you to recognise your strengths and key skills, looking for opportunities to use these each day. You are not just a cog in a wheel – who you are and what you do matters.

Mother Theresa said "I alone cannot change the world, but I can cast a stone across the waters to create many ripples." Don't underestimate the effect of believing in yourself and understanding your value.

Did you spot the 7 keys?

This is just the start, a brief overview of what is possible to reignite your passion for your role.

To find out more about Rowena Hicks' work, her training, videos and free worksheets from the book and more, go to linktr.ee/authorrowenahicks

P.S. Reviews are the lifeblood of independent authors. To help get this book into the hands of more readers, please leave a review wherever you bought the book!

References

Brené Brown (2010). The Power of Vulnerability and Courage to be imperfect.

Gary Chapman (2015). The 5 Love Languages.

Denis Haack (2015). When spiritual growth involves discomfort.

Patricia Eurich (2018). Increase your self-awareness with one simple fix.

Stephanie Marken & Sangeeta Agrawal (2022). K-12 Workers Have Highest Burnout Rate in U.S.

Mihaly Csikszentmihalyi (2018). Flow: The Psychology of Optimal Experience.

Maureen Gaffney (2015). Flourishing.

Peter Gibbon (2020). Martin Seligman and the Rise of Positive Psychology.

Simon Sinek (2010). How leaders inspire action.